CW00841670

To Elka   G.B.

Text by Sophie Piper
Illustrations copyright © 2009 Georgie Birkett
This edition copyright © 2009 Lion Hudson

The moral rights of the author and illustrator
have been asserted

A Lion Children's Book
an imprint of
Lion Hudson plc
Wilkinson House, Jordan Hill Road,
Oxford OX2 8DR, England
www.lionhudson.com
UK ISBN 978 0 7459 6160 6
US ISBN 978 0 8254 7907 6

First edition 2009
This printing December 2009
10 9 8 7 6 5 4 3 2 1

All rights reserved

A catalogue record for this book is available
from the British Library

Typeset in 34/40 Tapioca ITC
Printed and bound in China
by South China Printing Co Ltd

Distributed by:
UK: Marston Book Services Ltd, PO Box 269, Abingdon,
Oxon OX14 4YN
USA: Trafalgar Square Publishing, 814 N. Franklin Street,
Chicago, IL 60610
USA Christian Market: Kregel Publications, PO Box 2607,
Grand Rapids, MI 49501

Ready, Steady, Grow!

Sophie Piper * Georgie Birkett

LION
CHILDREN'S

Do you dream of growing taller?

Make yourself

small

and then   reach.

Still not taller?
Growing up takes time... and care.

First you need to eat good food.

vegetables
in all sorts of
colours

fruit in
different
shapes and
sizes

proper meals with all kinds of
good things in them

(not just sweets and snacks)

When you go out to play, choose the right clothes...

sun hat for sunshiney days

waterproofs and
boots for rainy days

hat and scarf
for chilly days

To help your body grow strong, you need to be active.

Do you like jumping...

Sometimes you must take extra care...

wear a helmet on your bike

keep away from the edge

don't go too high

It's more fun when you stay safe.

As you grow bigger and stronger, you will learn to...

climb higher

jump further

run faster

If accidents happen...

Oops

dab it clean

wear a bandage over the cut

Help your body to mend itself.

Do the things you love to do...

the things that make you happy.

At the end of each day, get ready for a new tomorrow.

wash yourself clean

brush your teeth and gums

Let your body get plenty of sleep

ZZZZZZ

You will grow as the days go by.

sunny days of summer

rainy days as winter comes

birthdays and party days,
festivals and fun

Look what has happened!

Everyone has grown in their own special way.

How do you measure up?

Remember to measure
1 foot or 30 centimetres up
from the floor and stick
the height chart in the
right place!

small is
good too